ENDORSEME

I love when people share things, when they feel so strongly about something that they want YOU to have it too! Rachel is a sharer! She wants you to know you CAN hear God but also shares HOW to!

Rachel is woman who has been in the written Word for decades! She knows the Word! In this new book, "He Speaks" she shares with you Biblical truth that people can and do hear God. She will walk you through a process that will deepen your intimacy with the Heavenly Father. This book will grow you in sweet ways and lead you into a deeper relationship with Him!

Winsome and deep, that is Rachel! Join her on the journey as YOU hear GOD in a fresh new way. You are in for a treat!

Gayle Novak. International Professional Coach and Speaker. G2G Discovery Coach.

Hearing the voice of God comes naturally to Rachel. If you know her and even if you're just meeting her, you'll quickly hear Scripture flowing from her lips, because it so beautifully flows from her heart. She has spent the majority of her life cultivating a listening ear by reading God's Word and obeying it.

Journaling also comes naturally to her—she's writing her thoughts to God and writing what she hears Him say back to her. It's like a sweet dance between a daughter and her daddy, as thoughts, ideas, prayers develop into words across the pages. Thank you Rachel for sharing the intimate sounds you've heard from the heart of our Heavenly Father. You are LOVED!

Lisa Dorr, Author of <u>Every Little Detail,</u> Radio Host, and Audiobook voiceover, who passionately loves Jesus.

"Rachel has authentically captured in He Speaks a wonderful key to intimacy with God. The value of the practice of listening to his voice and writing it down will benefit any believer. A must read!

Reverend Ron Roberts, Retired Lead Pastor.

I've known Rachel for 30+ years and have watched her grow from a young mom, wife, friend, artist and teacher who always loved God into a God loving, God trusting, God KNOWING daughter of the King who hears His voice as if she were His favorite. In her writing she teaches each of us who are daughters of the Most High God we, too, are His favorites and we, too, can hear Him speak into the the most personal areas of our lives as only the sweetest of lovers can do. She writes like she speaks - simple, funny, profound; and she encourages each of us To tune our ears and hearts to hear our Father just as simply and lovingly and as profoundly as His message is tooled to our own souls. HE SPEAKS! INDEED!

Sally Roberts

Rachel Inouye is not only "the real deal," she encourages others to find that same "God-fidence" that will enable them to be authentically and completely who God created them to be. Jesus oozes out of Rachel in every conversation she has, both verbal and written. She speaks truth to others because He speaks truth to her. He Speaks: Hearing the Voice of God through Journaling will guide the reader in that same authentic, life changing relationship with the Father as they learn to listen as He speaks.

Tabitha Deller
Bible Study Author and Teacher, Women's Ministry Event Speaker

As Rachel's cousin, I have had the privilege of watching her grow in her ability to communicate with the Lord. As she has stewarded listening to His voice, she has really grown and learned just how important it is not only to hear Him, but to recognize the difference between His voice and the voice of others. As a teacher, she is able to walk people through this journey in a way that is easy to learn and encouraging, along the way.

If you've ever struggled with hearing His voice, this book will bring you into new truths and break off the lie that not everyone is able to hear Him. Even if you hear Him well, this book will shed new insights into what you already knew and help you to grow even further into this process.

Annie Davis - Cousin, Blogger, BSSM Student

Over our 30 year friendship, I've watched Rachel grow in her love for God and in her appetite to hear His voice. Her daily practice of listening to Him and letting His great love pour out of her pen is truly her spiritual oxygen. On our travels together over the years I've watched her sit silently, journaling truths that the Spirit whispers into her soul. She's often up before the rest of us, drinking her coffee, with ear buds snugly in place, her bible open in her lap and her journal open to a fresh, blank page — awaiting what Father has for her that morning. And, without fail, the lover of her soul brings her to Himself through the listening journals she keeps. She treasures His words in her heart and savors them through writing. I'm so glad she's bringing her beautiful practice as a gift to the rest of us!

Lisa Harding
Friend, Advocate, Influencer

He Speaks

He Speaks

Hearing The Voice of God Through Journaling

Rachel Inouye

COPYRIGHT:

Scripture quotations taken from The Holy Bible, New International Version® NIV®
Copyright © 1973 1978 1984 2011 by Biblica, Inc. ™
Used by permission. All rights reserved worldwide.

Scripture quotations are from the ESV® Bible (The Holy Bible, English Standard Version®), copyright © 2001 by Crossway, a publishing ministry of Good News Publishers.
Used by permission. All rights reserved.

He Speaks Hearing the Voice of God Through Journaling
Copyright © 2020 by Rachel Inouye.
All rights reserved.

Cover design: Michael Heggen Inouye

DEDICATION:

For Michael.

For how you have supported me in everything I've ever toyed with, attempted, or done.

For being a wonderful provider, best friend, husband and my amazing forerunner! Without you, none of this would ever be a THANG!

You've edited and formatted our lives, not just this book. You make me radiant!

I love you always and in all ways.

Rachel

CONTENTS:

Forward	10
Prologue	14
Introduction	17
How To Use This Book	23
One	29
Two	34
Three	38
Four	42
Five	46
Six	51
Seven	55
Eight	59
Nine	63
Ten	67
Eleven	72
Twelve	76
Thirteen	80
Fourteen	85
Fifteen	89
Sixteen	93
Seventeen	97
Eighteen	102
Nineteen	106
Twenty	111
Twenty One	115
Twenty Two	119
Twenty Three	123
Twenty Four	128
Twenty Five	132

Twenty Six	136
Twenty Seven	141
Twenty Eight	145
Twenty Nine	150
Thirty	154
Thirty One	158
Acknowledgements	164
About the Author	172
Connect with Rachel	173

FORWARD:

This book, He Speaks, is being released during a global pandemic at a time when we are all trying to persevere. Rachel knows how to persevere in trials and storms and this book is for "such a time as this." (Esther 4:14)

I trust Rachel's character and integrity. She has learned what voice to listen to because she knows the word of God and this comes through in He Speaks. So we can listen to her.

Rachel and I met twenty years ago, when she walked into a bridal room adjacent to our church chapel to grab a tissue, because the worship music had moved her to tears. I was in the room getting a lapel microphone hooked on my blouse. I was to speak to the women gathered in the nearby chapel.

With her typical radiant enthusiasm, Rachel blurted, "Oh, I'm sorry, I didn't mean to bother you, I just need to grab a Kleenex. Hi, I'm Rachel Inouye and I'm so delighted to meet you Jill! I've heard you speak, over the radio, it was an interview with you, for Focus on the Family, with James Dobson. I remember your accent and the story of Achan, 'You can't Win the Battle with Sin in the Camp,' she continued to rattle on. "We've recently moved here from the Twin Cities and it will all be worth it, if only to sit under your teaching and preaching!"

We bumped into each other now and then and I'd see her upfront leading worship. But it wasn't until about ten years ago that our relationship became a friendship.

During a terrible storm in her life, which brought confusion and great loss, Rachel asked to meet with me. Even during those difficult times, she clung to God and remained hopeful. Her faith grew and was strengthened. The Father's sovereignty and goodness was never in question for her.

More recently, I've been a returning guest on Rachel's podcast, "the real deal" we never run out of stories or laughter, while recording the episodes. We plan to do more of them in the future. She is authentic, vulnerable and her self-deprecating humor immediately puts people at ease.

Rachel has a passion for God's word, it keeps her rooted in hopeful thoughts and she directs her life accordingly. Being a woman of the Word, she reads, teaches, and memorizes it. This dicipline and delight has allowed her to recognize the nature and character of God. Sitting with and listening to Him has developed her ability to know the voice of the Lord. Rachel knows her Bible and she knows-He Speaks! This is a timely work.

Rachel Inouye speaks and writes to: inspire, shift perspectives, equip others, ignite hope and to be a contagion for God's glory! She has the spiritual gifts of faith, encouragement and exhortation. Rachel celebrates others easily. She's a gentle, general in the army, equipping the saints of the kingdom and this book is written to encourage and equip all of us.

Jill Briscoe
Speaker and Author

~ This is an invitation into greater intimacy with God~ Rachel

Listening to His voice and journaling what I hear has become a treasured part of my faith journey. It's like the Miracle Grow® to the flowers in the garden of my heart.

The experience of reading this book and gaining ground in listening to the voice of God would be GREATLY increased by reading the Introduction - Hearing my heart, the catalyst behind writing this book.

When I'm privileged enough to walk alongside and help someone grow in intimacy with God, I get so excited I could do cartwheels! This book, <u>He Speaks</u> and the companion journal – <u>I'm Listening</u>, is a call to greater intimacy through listening and journaling. I'm excited for you to begin!

Rachel

PROLOGUE:

So many voices come at us daily, we must train ourselves to hear the voice of God and discern it amongst all the others that clamor for our attention.

I recognize I am one of the voices out there. I am Rachel Inouye, beloved child of the Most-High God. I am a gifted-communicator, story-teller, podcaster, speaker and author. One who has been talking, almost non-stop, since I uttered my first words. No joke! As you might imagine, "listening" came less easily for me because speaking is my jam!

I have however, honed the skill of listening to the voice of God for many decades and it is how I developed my own identity as well as talks I've presented to thousands of people. My identity talk, "I Know Who I Am!" has many elements to it and one section is all about the constant VOICES we hear in our heads.

I develop for each audience the need to distinguish between our own voice, the voice of the enemy, Satan and the voice of God. I know my Father's voice because of our relationship and time spent together. I've listened to his voice and have written down what I've heard him tell me. <u>He Speaks!</u>

The purpose of this book is not only to whet your appetite for hearing God but to help by giving you tools that I've used along the way.

Seriously, there is nothing better than to hear from and be in communication with Almighty God. We speak, it's called prayer and we listen, you guessed it, it is also called prayer.
Creating this book wasn't easy, nor was it excruciatingly laborious. I compiled multiple entries from my own journals, which you'll hear more about in the introduction. Would I like to inspire, sure! But I believe I am a catalyst for change. Change in behaviors, change in beliefs and even a change in life. If you do something different or become someone different through this process then I know Holy Spirit is working and it is all well worth it.

I'm convinced you will change and grow in your relationship with God, if you implement what I describe and lead you through in this book, <u>He Speaks - Hearing the Voice of God Through Journaling</u>. This may be a HUGE game-changer for you, I know listening the way I'll explain, certainly was and still is for me. This is a bit like fertilizing a garden and watching it grow. It is so exciting.

We know God speaks, Jesus is the WORD of God.

He speaks to us in His word the Bible, through other people, in creation, through music, via the anointing of preacher's sermons. Yet, we can train ourselves to listen to His voice daily. It's a relationship - so we listen to our Father's voice.

Jesus said: "My sheep hear my voice, and I know them, and they follow me." John 10:27

<u>He Speaks</u> - explains my process of listening: of stilling myself, focusing on Jesus then listening and writing down what I hear. (like the little boy Samuel…)

A third time the Lord called, "Samuel!" And Samuel got up and went to Eli and said, "Here I am; you called me."
Then Eli realized that the Lord was calling the boy. So Eli told Samuel, "Go and lie down, and if he calls you, say, 'Speak, Lord, for your servant is listening.' " So Samuel went and lay down in his place.
The Lord came and stood there, calling as at the other times, "Samuel! Samuel!" Then Samuel said, "Speak, for your servant is listening." 1 Samuel 3:8-10

<u>He speaks- Hearing the Voice of God Through Journaling</u> is an equipping /devotional book. It has 31 entries, which are actual typed pages from my own journals. Each entry is then followed by a:
- <u>Scripture to Embrace</u>
- <u>Question to Consider</u>
- <u>Prayer</u>
- <u>Declaration</u>

PLUS: An extra equipping part, as if I'm sitting with you saying, "*NOW YOU PRACTICE*" comes this section Write What You Hear: to the prompt I use myself- The LORD says My Love…

a blank page is also included for you, dear reader to practice listening and journaling on your own.

(*Remember all five senses and whatever you "get/hear" write it down. It could be a phrase, a picture, a smell, a taste, a song title…don't over think it, write it down.*)

When I have the privilege to walk alongside someone and help them grow in intimacy with God, I get so excited I could do cartwheels! This book He Speaks and companion journal-I'm listening, is my way to reach as many people as possible in this call to greater intimacy, through listening and journaling.

 I'm excited for you to begin!

INTRODUCTION

Please hear my heart and the catalyst behind writing this book.

I truly believe God sovereignly directs books into the hands of readers so it's not an accident that you have this book, He Speaks in your hands now. He knows you, He made you, He lavishly loves you, and He is speaking to you.

Keep reading for just a bit of the story behind this book. It's not only about my journey of hearing the voice of God through journaling, but He Speaks will model for you and further equip you as I walk along side you, so to speak. I'm confident you will grow. **This is an invitation into greater intimacy with God.**

"A man prayed and at first he thought that prayer was talking. But it became more and more quiet until he realized that prayer is listening." -Soren Kierkegaard

I am a doer and a goer and as my husband says, a flitter, so to sit down and still myself has taken intentionality and practice. Nearly two decades ago, I was challenged to sit and listen for the voice of God in prayer and then write it down and journal. I had a blue journal that was blank at the time so I started there, I called it my listening journal.

So Eli told Samuel, "Go and lie down, and if he calls you, say, 'Speak, LORD , for your servant is listening.'" So Samuel went and lay down in his place. 1 Samuel 3:9

I began to practice listening and journaling and found out that God **simply** wanted to say something. I mean simply! He wanted to say something to ME. He speaks!

I sat quietly with pen in hand, journal open and waited. I wrote the first thing I heard after I had written this phrase: *The Lord says, "My daughter…"* Whatever I heard, I wrote it down. It could be just a word, I wrote it down. Maybe I got a phrase, or only a short sentence, at first it was very brief but I wrote it down.

Typically, he would just say, *"I love you."* So I would sit there wondering, do you have anything else to say? Soon I found, as I sat each day and waited eagerly pen in hand, journaling whatever I heard in response to this phrase: The Lord says my daughter… And he'd say something again like, *"I love you."* Or *"I made you."*

What I heard evolved over time into writing down things like, *"I love you and made you, just be you!"* Looking back now, I realize the repetition was the way He was shaping my identity in him. I am lavishly loved by God and I know it… He's told me repeatedly.

I continued to practice listening to the voice of Father God. Often I would hear, *"Trust me. I'm right here."* Or *"I'm pleased with you."* After years of sitting and writing in what I called, "My LISTENING journals" I began to learn the sound of his voice and that He truly speaks to me. Yes, of course, He speaks in His word, through songs and preacher's sermons, in nature, through other people's lives and circumstances and situations too.

But I began to trust and rely heavily on Scripture and on what He said to me as I wrote it down each morning. I was drawn to His voice. I am a woman of the word, I read it, memorize it, sing it and absolutely LOVE it.
Years later, I decided to alter slightly the beginning of each journal entry. I started with this phrase, *The Lord says, "My love…* Not because I am no longer his daughter, but because I was so enveloped in his love. I am his beloved. Be loved. His perfect love was casting out fear and forming me into who I am today. He's making me more like Jesus.

Keeping this practice hasn't always been easy. I told some people about my listening journal once while I was speaking. I'll never forget it, after I finished my talk a woman approached me and chastised me for listening and then writing down my thoughts on paper.
She warned me that I can NOT hear God's voice other than from his word, the Bible. She sent me many articles and emailed me multiple things warning me not to sit and listen to God. So I put the listening journal away for some time, maybe about a year. I'm not certain.

Let me tell you what happened next, I began to dry up and wither on the vine. We all know that prayer is a conversation… Both talking to God and listening to him speak.
So, I picked up my listening journal again and practiced sitting and listening to the voice of God knowing and believing that He speaks. Whatever I heard, I wrote down in my listening journal, I grew like a plant in sunshine, with the Gardner watering me and applying Miracle Grow®.

I am glad I received that warning and I want you to know I never write down anything that I feel is contrary to the word of God. But I do write down personal things that he says to me.

Because I am in a relationship with Him. This book, He Speaks, is a devotional of sorts. It's about Him speaking and us hearing, if we incline our ear.

Some of the things I changed slightly, because I wanted to make them a little more general for you, the wider audience, but I think you'll understand even if I'm being specific to what He told me in my life.

For example, I may have written: *I have your children.* Maybe you don't have children, yet or won't have them but I think you can understand and get my drift.

My hope is that you, dear reader, will take the time and use this journal as a way to discipline yourself to simply sit with God and write what He says to you. It's an invitation to greater intimacy with God.

Warning: this is simple so don't judge it. Trust it and read each entry S. L. O. W. L. Y!

At the end of each entry I've given you some space to write things down on your own. You write what you hear when you sit and listen to His voice. Remember He SPEAKS.

In your mind, you simply write down whatever you get that comes to you. Maybe you'll hear a song lyric, or smell something, perhaps it'll be warm bread or the taste of honey. Maybe God is just telling you that he's the bread of life and that his word is like honey for your soul.

Don't let this freak you out, intimidate you, or tip you over. This is an experience. A time to be with God. It's a way to listen to His voice.

Hearing God's voice through journaling has been a rich time for me and I want to share with you. As you can see once you begin reading, my entries aren't profound, I don't use big words, that's because God speaks to me the way He speaks to me. Often God speaks to us and it sounds like our own voice. I hope that makes sense?

You see I've been given the mind of Christ. If you are in Christ, you have the mind of Christ as well. So His thoughts and voice sounds similar to your own. Since I don't use a bunch of big words God doesn't use a bunch of big words with me.

I hope you wouldn't judge or scrutinize the contents of this book, rather you'd read it or even speak it aloud and then begin to hear the Father's voice. I was challenged by a missionary friend from our church to do this exercise:

1. *Sit, Be still*

2. *Look to Jesus*
3. *Listen to His voice*
4. *Write it down.*

Years later I read a book by Leif Hetland, Called to Reign, while reading it I was encouraged by another format he suggested for praying and listening… He suggested we ask three questions:

Papa, what do you see when you see me? What do you feel when you feel me? What do you think about when you think about me? Some of the entries here have followed that format loosely. (You may use that too.)

My prayer is you will find your own groove as you hear His voice. Maybe you've done something like this for years, but if you haven't, I'd like to think it is beneficial to your walk with the Lord.

Honestly, I don't always write in my listening journal, I have other journals I use in response to the scripture that I've read that day. The listening journals are filled in tandem with the others to help me sit, wait and listen to God.

One thing I want to mention, NEVER stop reading the word of God. It is your food, daily bread and living water of the Holy Spirit. It is life.

We worship the Father, Son and Holy Spirit not the Father, Son and Holy Bible. I want an encounter and relationship with Jesus, Father and Holy Spirit. He speaks so I choose to incline my ear, listen and write it down.

I sure hope this helps you understand the catalyst for this book. I'm excited for you to begin. Thanks for trusting me enough to read this long introduction.

Like I stated in the beginning, I truly believe God sovereignly directs books into the hands of readers, so it's not an accident that you have this book <u>He Speaks</u> in your hands now! He knows you, He made you, He lavishly loves you, and He... is speaking... to you.

HOW TO USE THIS BOOK:

You may be wondering, so how do I use this book? Don't I just read it? Well, yes and... no! This book, <u>He Speaks</u> has thirty-one entries. That is intentional as I hope it will be habit forming. It may only take you a month to read and work through it. Great! Knock yourself out.

If you'd like to do the exercises that follow on a separate day it may take you two months. Just read, listen and reflect longer, if you'd prefer. This is at your pace. I believe that you will continue to hear God's voice and journal your encounters. There is a companion book called: <u>He Speaks-I'm Listening</u>

I'd suggest you read each sentence slowly. They're often stand alone thoughts but I've chosen to put them in paragraph form. I believe you will get the most out of this if, after you've read the section, you still yourself long enough to journal your own response each day to this prompt I've provided, *"The LORD says, "My love..."*

Perhaps you are already used to sitting and listening, you often practice hearing the voice of God through journaling, wonderful! Some of you may already be journalers. Terrific! But whether you're already a pro or this is new, I invite you to read this book and hear God's voice through stilling and journaling.

Try it! As you tune in or incline your ear as Scripture says, write down what you hear. I get the picture of someone leaning in to hear the whisper of another telling them a precious, tender truth or wonderful secret for their ears to delight in. They excitedly jot down what was said. Here's an example: "Hey, I love you!"

God speaks. It's a sure thing. Jesus is "THE WORD" so we know He didn't speak the world into existence and then become mute. He has a voice and He speaks. What does it sound like? Well...

Have you ever been driving in your car and you have the thought of someone you need to call because they've popped into your mind? I know I have. The voice sounds like me, but many/most times it is God.

I recognize there will be others of you, for which this may be foreign or completely new... I get that! My hope is that this book could serve as a way for me to come sit alongside you as you begin to explore inclining your ear to hear His voice.

I hope this helps you "HEAR" His voice. Remember to be aware of all five senses and don't over think...He speaks and it may come as:
- a single word
- a picture
- a vision
- a dream
- a phrase
- a mental clip, like from a movie
- something you smell
- or even become as a taste in your mouth.

Whatever it is, I encourage you to **write it down.** Additional space is provided at the end of each entry for you to fill out on your own.

I'd like to be of assistance and it will be kind of like I'm holding your hand. As you read each of my entries, remember they are what I was hearing at the time. I am believing the best for you as you begin hearing God's voice through journaling.

It's a process and I believe you'll get hooked. Make your prayer like the young boy Samuel,

"Speak Lord, your servant hears!" *1 Samuel 3:8-10*

Here's a quote from A.W. Tozer that I have written in the front of one of my listening journals:

"Lord, teach me to listen. The times are noisy and my ears are weary with 1000 ruckus sounds which continually assault them. Give me the spirit of the boy Samuel when he said to the Lord, 'Speak, for thy servant heareth.' Let me hear thee speaking in my heart. Let me get used to the sound of thy voice, that its tones may be familiar when the sounds of the earth die away and the only sound will be the music of the thy speaking voice. Amen."
From: <u>The Pursuit of God</u> by A. W. Tozer

Before continuing with "He Speaks" let me offer some hints on listening to voices. I wrote about them in a blog, Are There Voices In Your Head? I will share a portion of here:

So here are some of my thoughts about the voices in our heads. We must realize there's always an inner dialogue going on. You've heard it, right? Yes, there are voices in our head. We MUST learn to distinguish the source of the voices that we're listening to.

Here are some things to keep in mind:
If the voice is the voice of approval it is from God. If it's a voice of accusation it is from the enemy. If it is a voice of comfort and confirmation it is from God but if it is a voice of condemnation it's from the enemy. If the voice is based on behavior and your past it is from the enemy but if the voice is based on your purpose and your destiny it is from God.

God: Comfort & Confirmation   Enemy: Condemnation
God: Affirmation   Enemy: Accusation
God: Your position in Him   Enemy: Your Performance
God: Purpose & Destiny   Enemy: Your Past & Mistakes

- So with that in mind, realize there could be four voice sources:
- An Angel
- Holy Spirit
- Your spirit
- An ungodly spirit – or the devil.

So recognize the voice or even straight up ask Holy Spirit, "Is this from you? God is this you?" Remember the voice is NOT from Father God:
- If it does not bring you encouragement…

- If it does not tell you, you are loved…
- If it does not show you your future, which is bright…
- If it does not have kindness and comfort… Remember, even in correction God is good and kind.

Scripture tells us, it's His kindness that leads us to repentance.
So if the above list is the VOICE you hear - then it is NOT from God. When it comes to that kind of voice you must choose NOT to listen. I've told my audiences many times and I will repeat it again in this blog today at the request of my friend. We MUST:
1. Recognize
2. Reject
3. Repent
4. Replace

It's pretty simple. When you recognize it's from the enemy or voice you shouldn't listen to then reject the thought. Then reject the voice and don't give it any more head space or airtime. Third, you have to think again on a higher level. Think in a kingdom way, re-think on a higher level…in the heavenly places with Christ where we are seated. Ephesians 2 - you have to repent. BUT REMEMBER you can't leave the shelves in your brain empty because the thoughts from the negative voice will come flooding back in so you must replace those accusatory thoughts with the truth.

When I was painting a room, I was hearing all the voices about why I shouldn't be doing this or that. I needed to be writing a blog instead. Blah, blah, blah. I don't even want to write the garbage thoughts. I had to silence the voice. Recognize, Reject, Repent, Replace!

I had to replace it with truth. I had to say aloud, **"You know what? This is how I'm wired. Psalm 139 tells me I'm fearfully and wonderfully made. This is the way I roll. I may make my husband crazy, I may drive people around me nuts but I am keeping in step with the Spirit and today this is what we are going to do. We're going to paint this room!"**

I don't know what you're battling today. I don't know whether you're hearing the voice of condemnation or not. But I do know God is speaking to you and his words over you are words of LOVE. They are words conveying His pleasure with you because He made you. He wants you to know He is proud of you and He sees your circumstances and how you are pressing forward. He wants you to know you are an overcomer. He wants you to know greater is He that is in you than he that is in the world. He wants you to know no weapon formed against you will prosper. It may be formed but it will not prosper.

He hopes like nobody's business you know you can do all things through Christ who strengthens you. He wants you to know He is the friend that sticks closer than a brother. He wants you to know the righteous have NO FEAR of bad news. He wants you to know He will provide for your every need. He wants you to know you don't have to dwell on the past. (If you confess your sins He is faithful and just to forgive your sins and cleanse you from all unrighteousness.) He doesn't want you to dwell on things Jesus paid for on the cross. He wants you to leave the past behind and go forward in faith.

Okay, I guess I DID have something to say today and at the risk of ranting, I just want to leave you with the thought that you too can do the four "R's". Maybe it'll help you to remember Rachel said them and they all start with the letter "R"
- Recognize
- Reject
- Repent
- Replace

I wrote about this in my book <u>Lily Pads – Stories of God on Display</u>. Chapter Two - Identity and the Tooth Fairy. rachelinouye.org

Let me lead you in a prayer:
Father, help all of us recognize the voices that are coming in and help us to know if it's from you or not. Lord, if the voices we listen to are from an ungodly spirit or the enemy I pray, in the name of Jesus that we would reject them. Lord, we repent of partnering with any thought that is not the way you think about us or our circumstances. We repent of thinking on an earthly level when we are kingdom people.
We repent of partnering with the lies and the negative voice of the accuser. We ask you for forgiveness. Give us the ability to think again

on a higher level. Lord, I thank you for your word. Your word is the truth. We can replace any negative thoughts and lies we've believed with positive thoughts of what you think about us straight from your word.

Thank you for what you say about us that we are fearfully and wonderfully made. You never make junk and you have started a good work and are faithful to complete it until the day of Christ Jesus. We thank you, we thank you, we thank you, we believe you are doing a good work in and through our lives. I pray this, in Jesus name, amen!

ONE

The Lord says, "My love…

Whatever you think is difficult is NOTHING for me. Remember who I am – focus on me, I am God! With that in mind, your present circumstance will shrink down to the size of a grain of sand.

I am God Almighty, your deliverer. I want to deliver you from any sense of needing to control, needing to force my hand or orchestrate the outcome of anything in your life. I am Alpha and Omega – I know the beginning from the end. So rest in my embrace. Underneath you are My everlasting arms.

I can provide. I can redeem, I can save, I can unshackle. I can call out the dead and raise it to life. I can bless you abundantly, I can remove all the barriers that hold you back. I am your shield, your very great reward and your abundant compensation.

Don't limit me in your thinking. I can heal, I can restore and make my words come alive in you and to those you care about. I am the one in charge and I am good.

Fear has no place in your life, only faith remains. Disarm the enemy from your thinking with praise. Have no dread for the future. No dread, that is unbelief but I am working now and in the future.

Let me remind you - you will be the head not the tail. You will lend and not borrow. You will be above and not beneath. The enemy has been defeated. He is toothless and only roars. You will refute every tongue that accuses.

You are an over-comer! You, my child, are more than a conqueror in me, in Christ Jesus. Do you receive it? Will you receive what I am giving you? Will you take seriously all the plans and appointments I have for you?

Sit here in my presence and then take me into every room you enter. Usher me in well. I am bigger than any problem you face. So, do not be afraid, do not be afraid my child. I Am that I Am!

My yoke is easy, my child, My burden is light. You need to surrender it all. All means ALL. Just pray, praise and watch me show off.

Scripture to Embrace: *There is no fear in love. But perfect love drives out fear, because fear has to do with punishment. The one who fears is not made perfect in love.* I John 4:18

Question to Consider: Where is my focus? Is it on God or someone or something else?

Prayer: God help me to never shrink you. You are almighty and I want to live my life in full awareness of your goodness, majesty and power. Thanks for all you reminded me of today.

Declaration: "My God can do all things, I am safe within His love and I have the peace of God dwelling in my heart."

<u>Write what you hear</u>: The LORD says, "My love…

TWO

The LORD says, "My love…

I love you, you are mine. I know you are hurting. I am here with you and I am for you. You can trust me with your life, with your future, I go before you and lead you in triumphal entry.

I am light and there is no darkness in me. See what love I have lavished on you, that you should be called a child of God? Yes, that is who you are! Trust me today. Trust me with your future and all your tomorrows.

Because you trust me, I will use you to bring courage to others. They are seen by me. They are in process and I love them while in process! I am not so concerned with the destination as I am with our journey together. Remember to remain in me.

I am the Prince of Peace cast your cares on me, my child – I do care for you. Let my peace rule in your heart. Lift your head – gaze upon my beauty. See the glory of the Lord and bask in my presence.

Scripture to Embrace: *One thing I ask from the LORD, this only do I seek: that I may dwell in the house of the LORD all the days of my life, to gaze on the beauty of the LORD and to seek him in his temple. Psalm 27:4*

Question to Consider: What does it mean to me that there is NO darkness in God? In what ways am I hurting?

Prayer: Thank you for always leading me in triumph. Help me to remember to remain in your presence.

Declaration: "I am a person of great courage!"

__Write what you hear__: The LORD says, "My love…

THREE

The LORD says, "My love…

Do you see my goodness and steadfast love? Do you trust me to fight for you? Have you truly surrendered? I only want to do what is best for you… Do you believe that?

Come close, get to know me anew- I am only for you, I am never against you. I delight in you. I love to spend time with you my child. I have really good things planned because I am good.

You never need to worry or figure out how I will do the things that concern you; I have the "how" covered. Just keep close to me and listen to my voice. You are mine and I take care of my own. I will guide you in all your ways, all of them!

Scripture to Embrace: *I will instruct you and teach you in the way you should go; I will counsel you with my loving eye on you. Psalm 32:8*

Question to Consider: In what way do I need to get to know God anew? Is there a Name of God or an aspect of His character to explore? (Example: Lover, Provider, Protector, Deliverer)

Prayer: Lord, I trust you to fight for me. I give you the 'hows' of my life and how it will all work out. Thank you for reminding me that you have it. Thank you, Holy Spirit, for being my guide and friend.

Declaration: "God is for me not against me!"

<u>Write what you hear</u>: The LORD says, "My love…

FOUR

I am the best, I am the only. I am the one you need to look to my child. I have everything you need. Everything! Bring all your dreams and desires to me. I love you, my child. I truly do – you are my prized possession. I love you and I am pleased with you.

Let not your heart be troubled, neither let it be afraid. In this world you will have trouble, but take heart I have overcome the world. I am with you and I will make your paths straight.

You may feel as though you live in obscurity, but I see you and know everything about you and I love all of it. Anything missing from you I will give you. I am a refiner. The fruit of my Spirit is in you.

Pray to me. I have heard your cries. I am working in ways you do not and cannot see. I need you to trust my character. I am for you and not against you. I have really good plans for you. So good, you will be amazed.

Lay down your life. Cease striving and rest in me. The world will tell you, you have to work and strive, I tell you I am working on your behalf.

I love you. You are so beautiful. How could you not be, you are made in my image. I will give you my eyes. I will give you my eyes to see people the way I see them. I will give you my heart for people.

Scripture to Embrace: *For you are a people holy to the LORD your God, and the LORD has chosen you to be a people for his treasured possession out of all the people who are on the face of the earth. Deuteronomy 14:2*

Question to Consider: In what way(s) do I feel like I live in obscurity? Do I really? God knows me, and has memorized everything about me does that add a new perspective?

Prayer: Father, Thank you for loving and excepting me just as I am. Thank you for loving me enough not to leave me that way, but to make me more like Jesus. May the fruit of the spirit become more evident in my life every day.

Declaration: "I am God's treasured possession!"

Write what you hear: The LORD says, "My love…

FIVE

The LORD says, "My love…

I continue to work on your behalf. I see you and I know the desires of your heart. You can trust me, will you? Wait on me and put your hope in my word. My timing is perfect.

Tell others of my love and forgiveness for them. I have a plan for their lives too, just like I have a plan for yours. It is to prosper you and not harm you, to give you a future and a hope. What the righteous desire will be granted.

Can you find joy in me? I am near. My joy is your strength, child. In this world you will have trouble, but take heart, I have overcome the world. I satisfy you with good things. Open your mouth and I will fill it.

I love you and I am pleased with you, my child. I delight in you. You make me smile.

I call forth the dawn – I hold the waters of the seas in jars. I weigh the sands of the seashore on scales. I have store houses for the snow, hail and lightning. I am in charge of your life too. Jump into my arms I will catch you every time. I am a father who is loving, good, and kind. I know what you need and I will supply all of your needs.

Scripture to Embrace: *Since ancient times no one has heard, no ear has perceived, no eye has seen any God besides you, who acts on behalf of those who wait for him. Isaiah 64:4*

Question to Consider: Do I trust God's timing? In what situation will I trust that God acts on behalf of those who wait for him?

Prayer: God, I thank you and I claim this promise today: Draw near to God and He will draw near to you. Thank you for being near to me every day in every way and in every situation.

Declaration: "God is releasing great strength and wisdom for my family and me today."

<u>Write what you hear</u>: The LORD says, "My love…

in the big things and the small. — I
am communicating my love for you... to you.
Do not worry.

The Lord Says My Daughter, My Love ;—   10-30-13

I am right here as close as the air you breathe.
I am here draw near. I am strong, you don't
have to be. I delight to show my strength
in your weakness. Come to me sweet one
come dear child. Breathe — Let me
calm you with my love. My unfailing love.
My loyal, steadfast, faithful love
my HESED!

I'm in control — You needn't worry.
I can do more in one move of my almighty
hand than all your planning or dreaming
in your whole lifetime.

Don't resist me — Or my love for you —
Press into me. Come close so I can kiss
your head. I adore you. I delight in
you. I care for you. I'm here — you
needn't fear. Cease striving — breathe —

SIX

The LORD says, "My love...

I see your desire to "DO" so many things today. I see the good in it and I see the frenzy. Lay down your concerns of the day...Let's do it all together. I love to be with you, my child. I love our relationship.

I love it when you talk to me all day long. I love it when you sing to me. I love it when you concentrate on who I am for you. I feel such love and affection for you. I know you wonder about my nearness from time to time, but I assure you, I am closer than you will ever know. I dwell in you, by my Holy Spirit.

I think about you all day long and my thoughts of you outnumber the grains of sand. I can't take my loving eyes off of you. I see when you sit and when you rise. You are my beautiful masterpiece who feels my heartbeat and displays my glory. You are my delight, just like Jesus is. He lives in you, I am pulled toward the Jesus, in you. I love you both!

Scripture to Embrace: *How precious to me are your thoughts, oh God! How vast is the sum of them! If I would count them, they are more than the sand. I awake, and I am still with you. Psalm 139:17,18*

Question to Consider: Who is God for me right now? What part of his character or nature is He revealing to me today? How am I responding?

Prayer: Jesus, thank you that you are a friend that sticks closer than a brother. Thank you for your nearness to me. You promise to be close to the brokenhearted and save those who are crushed in spirit, thank you. Help me sense your presence today and bring it to others as well. Amen.

Declaration: "I am God's masterpiece! His eye is on me and I have His peace dwelling in my heart."

Write what you hear: The LORD says, "My love…

SEVEN

The LORD says, "My love…

Be happy, rejoice! I am right here. I will never leave you or forsake you. I see you right now and I have good plans for your day. Every good and perfect gift is from above. I love to give good gifts. Keep watching as I give them and be aware that I am the source. Then give thanks. I delight to show you my goodness.

I delight to be with you, my love. Trust my heart. My heart is for you not against you. You never have to be afraid, my child.

Peace I give you, my peace. Shalom – nothing broken, nothing missing, peace. I will calm the storms in your life I will bring peace to the raging seas of your mind. I am so good.

You only have one enemy and it isn't me, nor is it you, nor any flesh and blood. So pray for those around you. Invite me in. Let me come into the places you need help. Don't let the waves roaring cause you to believe lies about yourself, about your future or about your circumstance.
I am the victor! You fight from victory not for victory. You are an overcomer and more than a conqueror in me. Let my peace protect your heart and guard your heart and mind in Christ Jesus. Do not be anxious about anything today.

Scriptures to Embrace: *No, in all these things we are more than conquerors through him who loved us. Romans 8:37*

Every good and perfect gift is from above, coming down from the father of the heavenly lights, who does not change like shifting shadows. James 1:17

Question to Consider: Am I thinking of peace as a thing or as a person? Jesus is the Prince of Peace and offers me, not just peace, but *his* peace.

Prayer: God, I receive the peace that you offer me, right now, in my life and in every situation. I welcome the shalom of God - nothing broken and nothing missing, peace. Thank you, thank you, thank you! Amen.

Declaration: "God is all powerful and every season. I can have peace in the storm."

<u>Write what you hear</u>: The LORD says, "My love…

EIGHT

The LORD says, "My love…

Trust in me with all your heart. Do not lean on your own understanding. Acknowledge me in all your ways and I will make your paths straight. You are not in control, I am. You don't tell the seas where to stop, I do.

You aren't able to move in men's hearts, I am. Don't even let doubt arise within you. SHUT IT DOWN - Only believe!

Will you, look with eyes of faith to me, my child? Will you turn every concern and uncertainty into a prayer of thankfulness?

Will you stand back and see the glory of the Lord revealed? I want to build your faith. I am Jehovah Jireh - not I was once Jehovah Jireh! Believe.

<u>Scripture to Embrace</u>: *"Where were you when I laid the earth's foundation? Tell me, if you understand... When I said, 'This far you may come and no farther; here is where your proud waves halt'?" Job 38: 4,11.*

<u>Question to Consider</u>: What doubts am I dealing with today? What circumstances, situations or people am I trying to control? Release the outcome to God now.

<u>Prayer</u>: Father, thank you for making my paths straight and guiding me. Thank you for knowing my heart and searching it today. Your wisdom and provision is mine at request and I ask for both today, in Jesus name, amen.

<u>Declaration</u>: "God is sovereign and good... God is working everything out."

<u>Write what you hear</u>: The LORD says, "My love…

NINE

The LORD says, "My love…

I made the heavens and the earth. I alone stretch them out… Nothing is too hard for me. So, with that in mind, whatever is in your life that seems difficult, remember it is never too hard for me.

Just keep taking steps; a great deal of small steps make a path in a direction of my leading. Know that I am pleased. Yes, I will convict and I will correct, but know that I am well pleased. For my anger lasts only a moment, but my favor lasts a lifetime. Weeping may remain for a night, but rejoicing comes in the morning.

My favor rests upon you; it's around you like a shield. Revel in it… Soak it up! Delight in me! I am pleased with you, you can trust in my lavish love. I love you so much I sent Jesus, my son to die for you and my Spirit lives in you.

When I made you, I used combinations I have never and will never use again. So show off my design! I get the credit. Don't worry about designer clothes – you are the designer's model, my masterpiece. Enjoy being you and enjoy this day I made too.

Scripture to Embrace: *For we are God's masterpiece. He has created us anew in Christ Jesus, so we can do good things, he planned for us long ago. Ephesians 2:10 NLT*

Question to Consider: Am I enjoying being who I am?

Prayer: Father, it means the world to me that you are so pleased with me. Help me to remain in your love. Thank you that I can boldly approach you to get the grace and mercy I need in my life. You alone are good and I love you. Amen.

Declaration: "I am fearfully and wonderfully made. God did a good job when He made me. I am a masterpiece!"

<u>Write what you hear</u>: The LORD says, "My love…

TEN

The LORD says, "My love...

I am near. Nearer than anyone else. I am closer than your breath. I am the friend who sticks closer than a brother. You are mine. I made you and I love you. I have given you the mind of Christ. Remain in me and I in you and you will bear much fruit.

Remember, a part for me you can do nothing. Cast aside your pride and your expectations that you have of yourself and of others. Renew your mind, let me shape your fragile heart. I hold it in my capable hands.

Don't doubt my goodness or my personal care for you. Come into the light of my presence, my child. Let it shine on you. Take this light and shine it everywhere you go and with everyone you meet.

I am in you— Christ Jesus-the hope of glory. The same power that raised Jesus from the dead, my power, lives in you. Power is mine and I live in you. Let me display my power in and through you today!

Scripture(s) to Embrace: "Who has known the mind of the Lord? Or who has been his counselor?" "Who has ever given to God, that God should repay him?" For from him and through him and to him or all things. To him be the glory forever! Amen. Romans 11:34–36

"For who has known the mind of the Lord that he may instruct him?" But we have the mind of Christ. 1 Corinthians 2:16

Question to Consider: In my life, is there a place where God is shaping or reshaping my fragile heart?

Prayer: God, I invite you to shape my fragile heart. You are forming me into your image. Let it beat in sync with yours. Thank you for giving me the mind of Christ. I will think about myself and my life from your perspective.

Declaration: "I have the mind of Christ. God is displaying His power and glory through me today!"

<u>Write what you hear</u>: The LORD says, "My love…

~Hey, this is Rachel popping in to let you know I am proud of you for continuing to make the effort to:

Be still
Look to Jesus
Listen to His voice
Write it down

Remember: You may just get a word or phrase, that's fine write it down.
You may see a picture or smell something or even have a taste in your mouth. That's fine, write it down.

Bless you!

ELEVEN

The LORD says, "My love…

I am praying for you and the people and things that concern you and fill your thoughts that distract you. Do not reject or discount the prayers others are praying. Realize I am praying for you all. I ever live to intercede for you.

I am the God who makes streams in the desert rivers in the wasteland. Nothing is too hard for me. No family situation, no health concerns, no financial difficulty, no sin condition is beyond my abilities or loving gaze.

You can trust me to finish what I have started in your loved ones and in you. I am working all things together for your good and for my glory. You are going to be amazed at the wonders I am preparing for you.

I sense you want things to turn out a certain way. I ask you to surrender your "picture" of how things should look and yield to my perfect plan and wonderful design. Don't freak out and don't give up. I am working and you are going to be amazed.

Scripture to Embrace: *I am God, and there is no other; I am God, there is none like me. I make known the end from the beginning, from ancient times, what is still to come. I say, my purpose will stand, and I will do all that I please. From the east I summon a bird of prey; from a far – off land, a man to fulfill my purpose. What I have said, that will I bring about; what I have planned, that will I do.* Isaiah 46:9b-11 NIV

Question to Consider: Is there an area or situation in my life that seems bigger than God or too hard for Him to handle? Ask Holy Spirit to reveal it to you.

Prayer: Lord, I repent of any unbelief in my life. I pull down strongholds and any thing that sets itself up against the knowledge of you. Right now, I make every thought obedient to you Jesus. (OR- Write out a prayer of you own yielding to the Father's plan in your life. Remember His purpose will stand AND His plans are good.)

Declaration: "Therefore he is able to save completely those who come to God through him, because he always lives to intercede for them." Hebrews 7:25 NIV

<u>Write what you hear</u>: The LORD says, "My love…

TWELVE

The LORD says, "My love...

I love you. I have you. Whatever you do today know that I am right with you. You are never alone and we do all things together. Let my power course through you and you will see my glory manifested. I am a way-maker for those who need to know the way. I see you in your trials and in your joys.

I love your learning. I love how you are learning to trust in the waiting in the doubt and in the trials of life. I am working all things together for you. I am the God of revival, restoration, reconciliation, renewal and rebirth. I am always working and I am good.

Those around you need to know they are truly loved without conditions, without performance, and without striving. As you cease striving you begin thriving, in who I am and who I have made you be.

Freedom is on the other side of the battle to TRY to be good enough, close enough to God, smart enough for acceptance, pretty enough for the world, and pure enough for the religious. Freedom is found in Me.

Remind those around you that I love them and I think they are "to die for!"

Scripture to Embrace: *It is for freedom that Christ has set us free. Stand firm, then, and do not let yourselves be burned again by a yoke of slavery. Galatians 5:1*

Question to Consider: What areas in my life need: Revival, restoration, reconciliation, renewal and rebirth?
Have I released each of these to Father God?

Prayer: Father, thank you that you use my life to reflect your glory. I know we become like what we worship, so I worship you today. You are the focus of my heart. I rest in your goodness. Thank you for loving me. In Jesus name, amen.

Declaration: "I am God's beloved. So I declare, I will allow myself to be- loved today!"

<u>Write what you hear</u>: The LORD says, "My love…

THIRTEEN

The LORD says, "My love...

I am for you not against you. I will never leave you; I will never forget about you. You are MINE and I love you. I am near, I stick closer than a brother. You can trust me with your pain, your life, with your future, with your loved ones.

I am good and only good. I am light and in me there is no darkness. See what love I have lavished on you-that you should be called a child of God – that is what you are, my love. Trust me today. Trust me with tomorrow's assignments and obligations. I go before you so trust me with your future.

As you encounter people, I will give you words to speak. I am using you to throw courage on them. Let those you encounter know they are seen by me. They are in process and I love them while in process. You love them too, with my love.

Remember I am not so concerned with the destination as I am with the journey. Let's journey together. Remind those around you they can be with me. I am the Prince of Peace. I speak peace to the raging storms of your life. Cast your cares on me, my child, I do care for you. Let my peace rule in your heart. Lift your head – gaze upon my beauty. See the glory of the Lord and bask in my presence.

Scripture(s) to Embrace: *One thing I ask from the LORD, this only do I seek: that I may dwell in the house of the lord all the days of my life, to gaze on the beauty of the LORD and seek him in his temple. Psalm 27:4*

The LORD is close to the brokenhearted and saves those who are crushed in spirit. Psalm 34:18

Question to Consider: Since the LORD promises to be close to the brokenhearted, how, and in what ways, am I sensing him right now? I don't have to FEEL him to rely on the truth of that promise.

Prayer: Father, I thank you that you promise to be close to me when I am brokenhearted. I need that right now! You also promise to save those who are crushed in spirit, so I will not rely on my feelings but I will trust the truth of your word. I will stand on the truth of your word making my circumstance, feelings or situation bow to you rather that let them run the show. I will gaze up on your beauty knowing it will shift my perspective. Help me fix my eyes on you. Amen.

Declaration: "When I am brokenhearted God is close to me."

Write what you hear: The LORD says, "My love…

breathe deeply. Again breathe — 10-31-13
The Lord Says My Daughter, My Love...
Good morning! Sit close draw near. I
am here. I'm always ready to be with you
you are the one who needs to slow down
to recognize my presence, but I'm here.
I will settle on you like a descending dove.
PEACE be still - I calm the waves. I can
calm you too. Let my love wash over you.
Remember you could sink it the ocean of my
grace and love for you. You are mine. There
is no one else like you. I truly delight in
you. Enjoy today. Fold me into the whole
of it. Breathe deeply. Those are the breaths
I've allowed today!
I am your rest: Rest from weariness,
rest from worry, rest from the noise of
the world in which you live. PEACE BE STILL.
The Lord Says My Daughter, My Love...

FOURTEEN

The LORD says, "My love…

I am here. I will never leave you. I have my eye on you all the time… I am delighted with you. My child, I really do have all things that concern you, so you can relax. Rest in me, rest in my goodness. Don't let the enemy have one moment of satisfaction that he has robbed your joy.

Breathe in: restoration, healing, unity, peace, and my rest. Breathe out: worry, anger, bitterness, pain, resentment, and hurt. Do it again! Breathe in and out. Let go of your sense of control… Submit to my plan, my purposes, my timeframe, my will. Yield to me.

You can have an over comer's attitude. I have not given you a spirit of fear, but of love, power and self-discipline. Trust in me. Nothing is too hard for me. I keep all of my promises.

My Holy Spirit will always teach you and comfort you and remind you of things I have said. I see you and I love you. I promise to take what concerns you so you don't have to carry it. Breathe…Do not hold your breath.
I have everything that concerns you. I've got this. I've got you. I do!

Scripture to Embrace: *"Ah, Sovereign LORD, you have made the heavens and the earth by your great power and outstretched arm. Nothing is too hard for you." Jeremiah 32:17*

Question to Consider: What am I trying to take or keep control of right now and why?

Prayer: Father, thank you that who you are is who I am on the inside. Thank you for all the provision you have made for me to know you through Jesus and live in your love today. You are an amazing God.

Declaration: "God is working everything out."

<u>Write what you hear</u>: The LORD says, "My love…

FIFTEEN

The LORD says, "My love…

Come close and lean in. I am near to you. I am right here. I see you. I see every tear you cry, every encounter with a friend, every laugh that comes from your belly and every move that you make. Each day I delight in who I made you to be. You are mine – I love you!

I made you to be blameless, pure and holy, come to me, for my blood has cleansed you. I desire to make you strong, firm and steadfast. I desire to give you the joy of the Lord - because I am your strength!

Stand back and watch me work! I will release you from the bondage and decay. Keep praying, casting your cares and trusting in me. The victory that I have for you is better than you could ever ask or imagine.

My ways are higher than your ways, remember that. Trust in me and do good. I am right here, I can be found in the warmth of the sun, the chirping of the birds, the beauty of the flowers, the waves on the ocean, gently falling snow, the touch of a child and the cry of a baby.

Drink in my goodness and mercy today.

Scripture to Embrace: *Though he brings grief, he will show compassion, so great is his unfailing love. For he does not willingly bring affliction or grief to the children of men. Lamentations 3:32-33*

Question to Consider: What life situation or circumstance can I yield to the truth of God's ways being higher than my ways? How might that shift my perspectives or attitude today?

Prayer: Lord, thank you for being right here with me and seeing me. Thanks for another day! Fill me with your joy today and allow my strength to soar. Help me see you in everything around me as I drink in your goodness and mercy. Amen.

Declaration: "Stress and strife has no voice or power over me. Holy Spirit I welcome you to lead me today."

Write what you hear: The LORD says, "My love…

SIXTEEN

The LORD says, "My love…

Welcome back! My arms are always ready for you. Your schedule is never more important than the time we spend together. Be joyful always. I love you.

Your cares and obligations are beginning to crowd your mind, give them all to me. I will be with you as you plan and set your schedule. I order your steps and your future. There is no where you can go that I am not already with you. Include me. Let's get these things done together.

Don't worry, worry is sin. Be confident, your confidence comes from me. I know and made each of your children let me have them. Think of passing them to me, even though they are already mine. Give me their schooling, their friendships, and their futures. I've got them and I have you too.

Say close to me, listen to my voice. My message is different than the world's. You are my beautiful child. I have what concerns you, I have good plans.

Remember, I delight in you!

Scripture to Embrace: *Therefore I tell you, do not be anxious about your life, what you will eat or what you will drink, nor about your body, what you will put on. Is not life more than food, and the body more than clothing? Look at the birds of the air: they neither sow nor reap nor gather into barns, and yet your heavenly father feeds them. Are you not more valuable than they? And which of you by being anxious can add a single hour to his span of life? Matthew 6: 25-27 ESV*

Question to Consider: What concerns/worries fill my mind right now?

Prayer: Father, I repent of any worrying I've done. Help me to trust in your provision, protection, and plans. In Jesus name, Amen.

Declaration: "The God who takes care of the birds provides for me today."

<u>Write what you hear</u>: The LORD says, "My love…

SEVENTEEN

The LORD says, "My love…

Your hope is in me all day long. Remain in me and you will remain faithful. Give me your day and your agenda. Allow my Holy Spirit to flow freely through you. Pay attention to the still small voice within.

Hide my word in your heart, continue to look for me to speak to you in every situation and circumstance. I am always communicating my deep love for you.

I am the God who sent the two foxes in the cool of the early morning dew to greet you the other day. I see the tears you cry and I watch over you as you sleep. I can be found each time you open the word and as you come to me in prayer.

I am the friend who sticks closer than a brother. Draw near to me. Watch me work. Stand back and watch me work.

Scripture to Embrace: *My Sheep hear my voice, and I know them, and they follow me. John 10:27*

Question to Consider: What is the main way I am "hearing" God right now? (seeing, hearing, feeling, knowing... Him)

Prayer: Lord, thank you for being the God of the smallest details of my life. You know the number of hairs on my head and you know what my day holds. I invite you into all of it and increase my awareness of your nearness. In Jesus name, Amen.

Declaration: "God speaks to me. I will incline my ear...I hear His voice."

Write what you hear: The LORD says, "My love…

The Lord says My Daughter...
View me rightly... See me on
the cross crucified for you. See the pain
I endured. The suffering was for
you. See me dead and buried...
See me raised to life again.
I am the risen one.
Resurrection power is mine
and the same power that I used
to raise Jesus from the dead is
in you too.

Rejoice over the fact that you
are fully alive. Be victorious in
your attitudes and in your faith.
I am the object of your faith.
Cling to me, my word. Do not
be discouraged. Do not shrink
back from what I am calling
you to do. Mostly to be with me
and to follow me and to trust me.
I love you. I delight in you. You
are the apple of my eye.
You are my beloved. I died for you, to
bring you to the Father — embrace
the love I have for you.

EIGHTEEN

The LORD says, "My love…

Do not be afraid… I am with you. Hope in my unfailing love - I am with you. I delight to show my goodness to you. You are mine!

Continue to come into my presence. In my presence there is fullness of joy and in my right hand are pleasures evermore. The world: things, stuff, people and the praise of man, none of that satisfies.

I am the source of everything! I give you this deep peace that you sense today. It is not some peace, it is my peace. I am with you even into old age and gray hairs… I am your God.

Bask in my goodness and glory and reflect me to others. Let my light shine through you. You are my billboard!

<u>Scripture to Embrace</u>: *Now the Lord is spirit, and where the Spirit of the Lord is, there is freedom. And we, who with unveiled faces all reflect the Lord's glory, are being transformed into his likeness with ever-increasing glory, which comes from the Lord, who is the Spirit. 2 Corinthians 3:17, 18*

<u>Question to Consider</u>: Is there anything blocking me from wanting to come into God's presence today?

<u>Prayer</u> : God, thank you that in your presence there is fullness of joy. Help me to continue to come to you to receive it. Thank you that you never leave me or forget about me.

<u>Declaration</u>: "Today is a good day! The goodness and mercy of God follows me today."

<u>Write what you hear</u>: The LORD says, "My love…

NINETEEN

The LORD says, "My love…

This is a good season for us. I have so many plans for you. Many of your favorite things are going to come together. Remain in me and watch me work on your behalf. Find your peace in me. I am the Prince of Peace.

I have my loving eyes upon you. You my love are the fix of my gaze. Never doubt your significance in the world or in the ways you bless me by your worship and your tears.

O I love you so much and I love to spend time together. I know the burdens you carry. I know you have listened to the enemies voice of condemnation. You are not responsible for every difficulty or hard thing in your life. Remember you have an enemy, he comes to steal, kill and destroy. Your life has his finger prints on it with some loss, death and destruction.

But I have come to give life and life to the full. I am doing a grand reversal. TRUST ME. I know it doesn't seem possible, in the natural. Yet I am not bound. What seems impossible with man is possible with me! I alone am God.

You can trust me because I am good. Look at the ways I have been evident and blessed you in the last days, weeks, months, years, decades. Trace my hand of goodness. I am here. Hold onto your hat, because I am about to blow your mind. Let's dream together then watch me blow way past those dreams.

<u>Scripture to Embrace</u>: *The thief comes only to steal and kill and destroy. I came that they may have life and have it abundantly. John 10:10 ESV*

<u>Question to Consider</u>: In what ways do I doubt my significance?

<u>Prayer</u>: Now to him who is able to do immeasurably more than all we ask or imagine, according to his power that is at work within us, to him be glory in the church and in Christ Jesus throughout all generations, for ever and ever! Amen   Ephesians 3:20,21

<u>Declaration</u>: "God is working in my life and he has good plans for me!"

Write what you hear: The LORD says, "My love…

Hey, It's Rachel again checking in. I'm so proud of the way you've been working through this book, He Speaks.

Remember you may "hear" differently than I do and that's okay. It's important to steward whatever we get so we can grow and get more. So keep it up!

TWENTY

The LORD says, "My love…

Settle yourself and breathe. Be still and know I am right here. I am so near to you in this moment. I know everything about you and every thought that you have.

I know everything about everything you face in the circumstances of your life. I am aware and I care. You can cast your cares upon me because I care for you.

I am wondering, do you really trust me? I have good planned for you and I desire to sit with you alone in the secret place as you open your heart to me. Let me love you like no one else can.

But once you have experienced my great love, you will desire more and more. My love will flow through you, fill you and will continue to draw you back to me again. My love and my filling will allow you to minister to the world around you, full of my Spirit, my love, without lack.

You will be my filled vessel ready to pour out at any moment, anywhere, to anyone

Scripture to Embrace: *See what great love the Father has lavished on us, that we should be called children of God! And that is what we are! 1 John 3:1a*

Question to Consider: Is my heart open to God's love? Holy Spirit show me…Is there anything blocking me from experiencing His love today?

Prayer: Lord, I'm wondering how you can help me today? Will you show me your ways? I invite you in now. You care for me like no one else ever has or can. Thank you for your lavish love for me.

Declaration: "I am lavishly loved by the God of the universe… I live and move and BREATHE in him!"

Write what you hear: The LORD says, "My love…

TWENTY ONE

The LORD says, "My love…

Calm down, calm yourself, come sit and breathe, Be still and know that I am God. I see you. I see it all, and I love you. You are in my hands and I hold your hand. We are walking together in life. I love you my child, I truly do. You are so special to me.

The way you love people deeply and allow them into your heart is beautiful and it is from me. You don't have to worry about getting hurt, I will protect you. I will shelter your heart.

You just love. Love all those you see. Love them with my love. You don't have to pretend to not be hurt by rejection, but you do need to keep your love flowing because I am the source of your love. Let my love flow to those who deserve it in your eyes, and to those who don't. You are a conduit for my love.

Ask me to touch those around you with my love. Ask me for the knowledge and wisdom to love them well. Ask me how to be a better wife, mother, friend, because I will show you.

I am so proud of you! You have stepped forward into new areas that I have challenged you in and I will continue to help people through you. You are my sunbeam, so shine!

Scripture to Embrace: *Fear not, for I am with you; do not be dismayed, for I am your God; I will strengthen you, I will help you, I will uphold you with my righteous right hand. Isaiah 41:10 ESV*

Question to Consider: Is there an area in my life that I am trying to protect myself?

Prayer: Father God, you are my source of strength and my protection I need you today. Thank you for being with me. Amen

Declaration: "I am God's sunbeam and I love those around me well."

<u>Write what you hear</u>: The LORD says, "My love…

TWENTY TWO

The LORD says, "My love…

I love you, my child. I'm glad you wrote it down because I need you to see it on paper. My love is lavish, it is relentless, it is massive and it is flowing freely.

You do not know what to do about this trial you face. I get that. You do not need to know what to do. Remain close to me. Trust that you are doing the right thing. You are loving those around you. You are loving me and you were releasing your cares.

One day, this trial, circumstance, situation… Will be resolved! Things will be redeemed and fully restored. I will deliver you from the fowler's snare and from deadly pestilence. I will. Remain in me as I remain in you.

I know it's hard at times. I know you are so relational - I made you this way. Embrace everyone you know. Show them love and appreciation before they have done anything for you. Love, love, love them.
I will use this love in great and mighty ways, doing great and mighty things through you because I am great and mighty. I am always working and you will make it through! A bent reed I will not break and a smoldering wick I will not snuff out.

I am for you and not against you. I am the fountain of every blessing. I am pouring out my spirit upon you. I am good! Watch me surprise you. Watch, you will see my goodness so keep watching.

Scripture to Embrace: *Though the fig tree should not blossom, nor fruit be on the vines, the produce of the olive fail and the fields yield no food, the flock be cut off from the fold and there be no herd in the stalls, yet I will rejoice in the LORD; I will take joy in the God of my salvation. Habakkuk 3:17,18 ESV*

Question to Consider: In a time of trial where am I positioned? Am I near to God?

Prayer: God thank you that you aren't trying to break me or snuff me out. Thank you for upholding me today, right now and in this moment. I rest in you. In Jesus name, Amen.

Declaration: "No matter what is happening, I choose to take joy in the God of my salvation."

<u>Write what you hear</u>: The LORD says, "My love…

TWENTY THREE

The LORD says, "My love…

I feel your confusion at times. Confusion is not from me. I feel your heart is heavy from time to time. I know and I feel it too. I want you to know how I see you.

I see you as an overcomer when we stay together and you abide in my love. Oh, how I love you! You are my beloved daughter and I delight in you. I will never leave you alone.

I think you have much to give in the way of helping others be "in me" and not be driven by being "in their circumstances." So, I say to you, move forward on your knees.

Lift your eyes to the hills…Where does your help come from? Does your help come from the mountains? No, your help comes from me, the LORD. I am the maker of Heaven and Earth, I have made you and I am making your life as I shape you in it. Come be with me, I am the potter, dear you're the clay.

<u>Scripture to Embrace</u>: *I lift up my eyes to the hills— where does my help come from? My help comes form the LORD, the Maker of heaven and earth. Psalm 121:1, 2*

<u>Question to Consider</u>: How do you see yourself? An overcomer?

<u>Prayer</u>: God, I need you. Help me look at my life through Jesus instead of looking at Jesus through my life. Give me the grander vision. Amen.

<u>Declaration</u>: "I have peace in the midst of the storm. I am never alone. The maker of the universe is with me. I am an overcomer!"

<u>Write what you hear</u>: The LORD says, "My love…

The Lord says my daughter...

Trust me, trust me, trust me. I am all that you need. I am more than you can imagine. My resources do not run out and I have the power and knowledge and ability to work wonders in your life. I can guide you through your break away talk. I will guide you if you are to move to Florida. I will not abandon you during this school year. I am still with you. Do not be anxious about your life, but live it. Enjoy your husband and kids, laugh, love and encourage. Commit your plans to me and they will succeed. I delight in you my sweet daughter. I desire to spend my time with you. Open the door of your heart I will come in and sup with you and you with me. Let's continue to deepen our intimacy.

TWENTY FOUR

The LORD says, "My love…

I see the tears of sorrow your heart has gone through. I delight to show you my forgiveness. I know you still feel pain and desire unity. That's my heart for you as well.

I feel your anger toward the enemy who has come to steal, kill and destroy. I feel you rising up on the inside to declare, "No more!"

Yes, the enemy has stolen from you. I came to give you authority to take back and reclaim and demolish strongholds and anything raised against the knowledge of God. Now you must take every thought captive and make it obey Christ.

You can't even imagine how beautiful all this will be. I work all things together for good in your life. You know , full well, that the enemy comes. BUT I have come to give you life and life to the full.

The best is yet to come so do not live in the past. The future is going to eclipse your past. I am the God of reconciliation and restoration and I am good. I am working in your life and in the lives of your loved ones too. Nothing is too hard for me.

<u>Scripture to Embrace</u>: *Behold, I will send you Elijah the prophet before the great and awesome day of the LORD comes. And he will turn the hearts of the fathers to their children and the hearts of children to their fathers, lest I come and strike the land with a decree of utter destruction. Malachi 4:5,6*

<u>Question to Consider</u>: What thoughts are coming in today? Should I embrace them or take them captive?

<u>Prayer</u>: Lord, help me as I snatch my thoughts and make them bow to Jesus. Your thoughts and plans for me are good. You desire and are working toward unity in homes, marriages, families, the church and in the nations. Thank you, I worship you!

<u>Declaration</u>: "God is turning hearts around, even mine!"

Write what you hear: The LORD says, "My love…

TWENTY FIVE

The LORD says, "My love…

Do not fret. It is sin. Anytime you fret it is rooted in unbelief. I have your family, your finances, your future, your health, your friendships and your marriage.

Trust in me with all your heart and do not lean on your own understanding. In all your ways acknowledge me and I will make your path straight.

I will keep you in perfect peace when your mind is stayed upon me and because you trust in me. I am able to do great and mighty things in your life and the lives of the members of your family and the many people around you.

Continue to come to me and rehearse what you know to be true, don't ever waver or shrink back. Claim my promises as your own. That is why I have promised. And what I have planned, that will I do.

Look back at my faithfulness and you'll trace my hand of grace upon your life. I am good. I am here, you need never fear.

Scripture to Embrace: *You keep in perfect peace him whose mind is steadfast, because he trusts in you. Trust in the LORD forever, for the LORD the LORD himself, is the Rock eternal. Isaiah 26:3-4.*

Question to Consider: Where and in what situations in the past have I seen God at work? Write them down, trace His faithfulness, see His track record with you.

Prayer: Jesus help me keep my mind on you. You are the Prince of Peace and I receive your peace now. Thank you, Amen.

Declaration: "I declare, in every situation, God's peace is available to me. So I am kept in perfect peace."

<u>Write what you hear</u>: The LORD says, "My love…

TWENTY SIX

The LORD says, "My love...

Come here, let me remind you of who you are. You are mine, you are forgiven, accepted, loved, holy, chosen, adopted, blessed, sealed and you are creative, funny, friendly, resourceful and faith-filled.

Continue to come to me daily, hourly, moment by moment to express your needs, your thoughts and concerns. Yes, I already know them, but I love to have you with me to express them and release those cares you have about..._____.

Cast your cares upon me - for I care for you. Lay your burdens down at the foot of the cross and leave them there. Do NOT pick them back up as you walk away! Believe me when I tell you, I work on behalf of those who wait for me.

My child, you keep trying to figure everything out and HOW I will work. But I am *God* let me do the impossible, you just do the trusting. That is what you need to do. Remain, stay and abide. Praise me, seek me, come toward me and never away from me. I love you and I care for you.

<u>Scripture to Embrace</u>: *Humble yourselves, therefore, under the mighty hand of God so that at the proper time he may exalt you, casting all your anxieties on him, because he cares for you. I Peter 5:6,7 ESV*

<u>Question to Consider</u>: What burden am I trying to pick back up or take back after I've given it to God?

<u>Prayer:</u> Lord, thank you for reminding me again of who I am in you. I rest in who you say I am and what you are able to do. Forgive me for trying to run the show. In Jesus name, Amen.

<u>Declaration</u>: God works on my behalf, I am loved and cared for by the LORD of lords.

<u>Write what you hear</u>: The LORD says, "My love…

~Hey, It's Rachel here to encourage you!

You're well on your way to completing this book. I hope you've been enjoying it! Are you aware of how you've been making progress? Keep practicing the art of listening to God!

I know the Father, Jesus and Holy Spirit are enjoying it. Your are the apple of God's eye and He loves you so much he wants to connect with you in deeper and more intimate ways.

Keep it up, I'm so proud of you.
I celebrate your journey. ~

TWENTY SEVEN

The LORD says, "My love…

Listen to my voice speaking to you in the smallest ways. Watch for me too. How closely will you pay attention? You will notice I am in every detail of your life; I am sovereign and completely in control of it all.

I'm in the places, with the people, present in the events, I have built the dreams of your life, and those of your children as well. I direct those things, so release all of it to me – I am able, well able.

You can trust me to take your hands and lead you - that's what I do. Will you trust that? Do you believe me? Will you follow? What if where I lead is not where you had imagined? I will still be with you.

Trust me because I have good plans for you. Do not be afraid. Fear is not from me. Live in faith, looking forward to what I have planned. I make your paths straight, bright and smooth. I make a way even when you are uncertain, I the LORD do not change. As so many things shift and change remember, I do not.

<u>Scripture to Embrace</u>: *I will lead the blind by ways they have not known, along unfamiliar paths I will guide them; I will turn the darkness into light before them and make the rough places smooth. These are the things I will do; I will not forsake them. Isaiah 42:16*

<u>Question to Consider</u>: How have I noticed God working in my life lately. Am I paying attention and following?

<u>Prayer</u>: Lord I've been uncertain lately. Help me understand more fully, along unfamiliar paths you promise to guide me. Thank you for making rough places smooth. I praise you. In Jesus name, Amen.

<u>Declaration</u>: "I never have to be afraid or chart my own way. God leads me in paths of righteousness for His namesake."

<u>Write what you hear:</u> The LORD says, "My love…

TWENTY EIGHT

The LORD says, "My love…

You are mine. I take care of my own. The plans I have for you are good and my love for you is unfailing and everlasting. Remain close to me. Remain in my love. Rest in it right now…pause and rest.

My glory is central in your life. Remain in me and lead others to remain close as well. Help others see and savor the glory of God all around them.

Make me central in everything you do. It is not about you, it is all about me! I am the Alpha and Omega, the one who made the world and everything in it. I have established my throne and my kingdom rules over all.

<u>Scripture to Embrace</u>: *The Lord has established his throne in the heavens, and his kingdom rules over all. Psalm 103:19*

<u>Question to Consider</u>: Is God central to everything I do?

<u>Prayer:</u> Father, forgive me for ever making things about me. I repent and will think on the higher level of your truth. Jesus you are the center of everything and you hold everything together…even me, right now and I thank you. Amen.

<u>Declaration</u>: God takes care of his own, I am God's…Therefore I declare: "God takes care of Me!"

<u>Write what you hear</u>: The LORD says, "My love…

(The Lord Says my Love...) Oct 18, 2011

Remember that I care for the birds...
I definitely care for you.
Trust in me with all your heart and
do not lean on your own understanding
in all your ways acknowledge me —
I *will* make your path straight.
   Come let me have a look at you —
I care so much for you. I love to be
with you. My Spirit lives in you. Let my
light shine through you — Come to me
I'm the Source of all the goodness in
your life.

(The Lord says my Daughter, my Love Oct 19, 2011)

Come to me do not hide. There is no
shame. You can come boldly to the throne
to receive the grace and mercy you so
desperately need. I care for Michael,
I'm the one who made him — I designed
him — I gave him his skills, talents,

TWENTY NINE

The LORD says, "My love…

I feel your heart yearning for more of me. I am your guide. I am your good guide.

I think you are in the hungry stages of yearning for more of me. You are verifying, through your life, that I will come through for you intimately, personally and willingly every single time. I think you've proven you are more in love with me than you ever knew.

Now you are realizing none of the other stuff really satisfies you. I think you need to wave goodbye to the old you. You need a new wine skin for this new wine I am pouring out for you.

I say you are powerful. You are mine a special treasure one the world needs to see on display. You shine like the stars in the universe as you hold out your light of life. You are an unstoppable force because of the power within you, my power!

You are my witness to the end of the age until the ends of the earth. I have made you on purpose for a purpose.

Scripture to Embrace: *I am the LORD your God, who brought you up out of Egypt. Open your mouth and I will fill it. Psalm 81:10 NIV*

Question to Consider: What are the things the world is serving that I no longer desire? What doesn't satisfy?

Prayer: Father God, thank you that you are the only thing that satisfies my soul. Help me to run to you each day. Help me to go to your word for it is like honey from the honeycomb to my lips. Thank you that you give me new wine, fresh bread, and satisfy my every need. Amen.

Declaration: "I am God's special treasure and He delights in me. He satisfies my soul."

Write what you hear: The LORD says, "My love…

THIRTY

The LORD says, "My love…

Come to me always. I am here with you and I am waiting for you. Never be afraid to enter my presence. The veil has been taken away, the curtain has been torn in two, from top to bottom, giving you full access to me.

I want to use you for my glory. Will you trust my plans, ways, timing and methods? I orchestrate things in a way you would never know.

Support those around you for my purposes to be advanced in their lives. Your husband, your children, your friends, your parents. They are a gift that comes from me. Enjoy them today. Be with them and give freely to them. I have ALL of those you care about in my safekeeping.

Clouds and thick darkness surround me, that is why you can't always see what I am doing, but no one can stop me. What I have planned that will I do.

REST, HOPE, TRUST.

Rest in me and my love for you. Hope for tomorrow and today because I am working. Trust that I know what is best more than you do – you may think you know, but I know better. Let it go, I've got you, just let go.

<u>Scripture to Embrace</u>: *For we do not have a high priest who is unable to sympathize with our weaknesses, but one who in every respect has been tempted as we are, yet without sin. Let us with confidence draw near to the throne of grace, that we may receive mercy and find grace to help in time of need. Hebrews 4:15,16*

<u>Question to Consider</u>: What practical thing could I do today that will help support the purposes of God in someone's life? (Husband, Child(ren), Parents, Pastor, Leader, Friend) Write it down and do it.

<u>Prayer</u>: Help me not to view you through my circumstances but view my circumstances through you. Help me to place all my hope in you, rest in you and trust you. In Jesus name, Amen.

<u>Declaration</u>: "I am filled with joy and peace. The God of hope is doing it, right now as I am believing Him."

<u>Write what you hear</u>: The LORD says, "My love…

THIRTY ONE

The LORD says, "My love....

I am your way maker. Stop trying to make your own way. I've got you and I've got "IT." Whatever your "IT" is, my child, I've got it. I hold your future and I have dealt with the past.

I love you with an everlasting, unending, unconditional love. You can't earn it, you can't ignore it and you can't disqualify yourself from it. You are the object of my love and I love to lavish it upon you. My perfect love casts out fear. You never have to be afraid.

Will you trust me with the things you think you need to accomplish and with the timing of miracles you are praying for to be realized? I am working all things together for your good. I'm delighted you are beginning to see that more clearly.

I am molding you and shaping you and peeling back layers of hurt, pain, mistakes, judgment, pride, religion and control. The fruit of my Spirit is taking over in your life. I am making you more like Jesus and it is beautiful.

Scripture to Embrace: *Therefore I tell you, do not be anxious about your life, what you will eat or what you will drink, nor about your body, what you will put on. Is not life more than food, and the body more than clothing? Look at the birds of the air: they neither sow nor reap nor gather into barns, and yet your heavenly Father feeds them. Are you not more valuable than they? Matthew 6:25, 26 ESV*

Question to Consider: What is the "IT" in my life today? Have I trusted my Father with it?

Prayer: Thank you, God for taking care of me. Thank you that whatever concerns me concerns you. Thank you that I can cast my cares on you because you care for me.

Declaration: "I cast my cares on God because He cares for me. I live free from worry and anxiety."

Write what you hear: The LORD says, "My love…

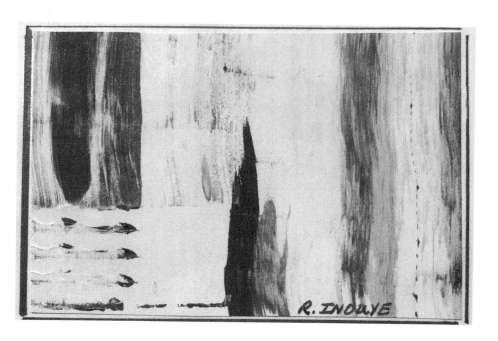

~Hey, It's Rachel, Congratulations, you made it to the end of the book!

But we'll never come to the end of encounters with the Father or His voice of love. I hope you will continue to practice hearing the voice of God through journaling. If you'd like you can start back at the beginning and continue to add to your listening entries.

If you still have room on the blank pages use them or go get yourself the companion listening journal, <u>I'm Listening</u> and use it for the purpose of hearing from God

"My sheep hear my voice, and I know them, and they follow me." John 10:27~

I'm all about getting people to God and equipping them too.

If you already purchased the companion journal to this book, now would be the time to pull it out and begin writing in it! Keep the momentum going and continue to hone the skill of listening to God's voice...He Speaks!

If you haven't yet picked up the I'm Listening journal, no worries, you may order it today if you'd like!

Acknowledgements:

Michael E Inouye - You have displayed patience as I continued to add to this book without any eye-rolling, even though it caused more work for you. I am impressed by how you tackle new and difficult things, like a boss! You are motivated by a challenge, it's like breathing oxygen for you. Babe, you've got mad-skills. I'm in awe of your perseverance in life and in any process. Thanks for seeing this book <u>He Speaks</u> through to the end. You are my steady-Eddy! You've been holding my hand for what seems like forever and I wouldn't want it any other way. I love you always and in all ways!

Michael Heggen Inouye - Son, you're the one with an ability to both hassle and hug me like no other! "Mom, I could snap you like a chicken!" Or "Ah, anaconda squeeeeeeeeze!" Your support of me and for this book means the world. Who else willingly returns a phone call at night after running seven miles playing ultimate frisbee? Your willingness to work on cover-art and the tweaks needed without complaining or even showering beforehand is a sign of your steadfast and agreeable nature. You are good-natured, kind, t
ender and you delight my heart. I respect you highly and love you deeply.

Amy Inouye - You are a woman who conducts herself with such thought, precision and poise. I stand back and marvel. You also allow me, from time to time, to pop your personal-space bubble and you handle it with utter grace. You love my son incredibly well, thank you! I'm truly grateful for you.

Andrew Inouye - As a red-cheeked, black-eyed toddler, you squealed with delight and jumped up and down in your crib whenever I entered the nursery. You have been jumping up and down in support of me ever since. I am truly touched. You're still a real cutie as adorable and handsome as ever. It might seem odd, but I'm thankful for LA traffic because you call to check in often. "So, how are you doing Mommy? Oh, that's great! I'm really glad you did that, I'm happy for you. Well, I just called to tell you, you're a good mom." Only a few of the phone sound bites that play like sweet melodies in my ears. You know how to volley in conversation and I have learned from your perspective on things. Andrew, you "see" people and love them wherever and however they are, it's one of your super powers! You'll never lose it. You're a rare gem and unique soul! Thanks for composing music for this <u>He Speaks</u> audio project. I appreciate who you are and who you are becoming. I love you!

Grace Elizabeth - I love you forever, like you for always, as long as I'm living my daughter you'll be. You are a light! Doing anything together, unloading the dishwasher, zipping down the produce isles, singing harmony, just hanging out or sipping coffee with you… whatever, it's a blast. I thank God everyday for the gift of you. (No joke!) I love you like crazy!

The Inouye clan: Robert† and Muriel Inouye, Anna Inouye†, Nancy Yang, Ken and Susan Tarter, Rob Inouye, Terri Inouye, Lance and Mickey Reisetter. Bob, I miss your voice. Thank you for always having the welcome of God on your life. Anna, I miss your feistiness and the way you spoke my name. I'm sure you're eating ice cream in Heaven! The rest of us are spread across five states, yet each of you are important to me. Who I am today as been enriched by our precious time together. Come visit! The global pandemic sure cramped our style…we still need some sort of reunion. Remember, I'm the ideas gal not the best candidate for executing the plan! I love you!

To my Mom, Lorraine Heggen, I don't know anyone else who intercedes in prayer like you do. The multiple notebooks you've filled with names, dates and details of the lives of those you bring before the Throne of Grace could fill countless shelves. I am humbled yet inspired by you. I'm a grateful recipient of your tender care: snickerdoodle cookies, caramel rolls, raspberry jam, taxi driving, constant love and continued prayers. You are constant, like God. You inspire me and I love you!

Dad, Richard Heggen you are "RD" the real deal. Your influence didn't only help me name my podcast, "the real deal" it helped form the essence of me. Good dads help form a child's identity, while providing and giving them a sense of purpose. Thanks for giving me all three…I hit the jackpot with you! Thanks for demonstrating the art of storytelling, I hang on your every word masterfully crafted and delivered. "Some people sure can tell 'em!" You are one of the most creative and inventive people I know. You remain personally motivated and catapult others into motion by your example. I believe it comes from sticking with the creator God...Who else has original hand painted walking sticks line their kitchen breakfast nook? You've been so supportive of not just me but Michael too! You have poured into Michael, Andrew and Grace so well. Your godly guidance, love and support is a great gift to me. Dad, you're my hero and I love you!

Barb Alcott- You are a hoot! The joy you bring to me, and to the world, is immensely needed. You being yourself is like a breath of fresh air to a closed up, musty room. No one else I know has an outlook on life or phrases that could immediately be sold and written on the fronts of humorous greeting cards. You crack me up! I'm proud to be your little sister and I've always looked up to you. The devotion to your family and the way you keep pressing forward in hard situations is compelling. You rock!

Craig Alcott - I am glad you married in...who else could handle Barb's exuberance? You love and accept each of us and have been such a good brother-in-law and a real "son" to mom and dad. Thank you for being you!

Sharon Romsey you carry yourself like you're walking the red carpet headed into the Oscars. You'd win the award for something related to beauty, costuming and set design. You reflect the artistry of our father Richard and Father God. Some of my favorite outfits are your gracious hand-me-downs. You have great taste! Thanks! You get more done in a month that I do in the whole calendar year. I know you'll never fully understand the way you have been the backbone of support to Mom and Dad. Being far away isn't easy. I so appreciate the multiple times you make a run for more vanilla bean ice cream and do the happy delivery to satisfy Mom and Dad's cravings! The regular support you provide our parents, your own family and mine is amazing. You have been so strong in the wake of great loss. I'm so proud of you! I love you.

Steven Romsey†...I miss you everyday. Your love for me and mine was never in question and it was unending. I always felt your smile upon me. It's a clear picture of how much God loves. Thanks for giving me that example of unconditional love. I know I'll see you one day!

Joyce Hansen - You have a shepherd's heart and the compassion and care you display makes me sometimes wonder, "Do I have a pulse?" You display the heart of the Father and the welcome of God is all over you dripping like thick honey. If you could, you'd feed the world and make the plate more appealing than any five star restaurant! While growing up, I guess we used to fight sometimes. I don't really remember it. Now all I know of you is, you fight FOR me never against me. Thanks so much. I love you big sister. I am so grateful God gave me you. I've watched you champion, value and notice people. God notices how you do that and He's well pleased with you. Love you so!

David Hansen - When you go for something you are all in Baby! "Let me put this in perspective for you" is something you say a great deal. You frame things like no one else, you're both a promoter and one full proclamation! God has and will continue to use your excitement to tell and sing truth. Thanks for always supporting me and this book too! It's been helpful.

Annie Davis - We find ourselves on the same family tree as cousins and you are also my beautiful sister in the Lord. You've employed unparalleled administrative skills with your love of checklists, tasks and deadlines. You reflect the glory of our ordered God. This book, "He Speaks" and the social media launch team have your fingerprints all over them. Thank you for doing what you do so well. Praying as mamas has brought us together but more than motherly concerns have reached the ears and heart of King Jesus. Love you bunches! This is an Ephesians 3:20 thing!

Lisa Harding - Should I call you Lisa or Barnabas? You are such an encouragement to me. Writing a book isn't easy, but once I decided to go for this one, "He Speaks" you were there with texts and excitement! (*"Sooooooo...I just love you. I'm so excited about your new book and LOVE how God just whipped it up out of the affair you two have together."*) The encouragement texts like this one were timely and wonderful wind in my sails. You are such an advocate for many and me...I sure do love you!

To my CABIN family: I love each of you so much. Scott and Lisa, Brian and Stefanie, Lane and SueAnn along with all the children and grandchildren born from our four families - Flom, Vaughan, Chandler and Inouye. I acknowledge you. We have bonded together because of Jesus Christ and his design for the body to live in community. We all, at one time, attended Grace church in Edina, Minnesota where the slogan was prophetic, "Where Friends Become Family" that sure held true! (All eating together what a wonderful...)

When I'm with you, I'm aware I am surrounded by greatness in the kingdom. Thank you for your constant love through the good, the bad and the ugly. I've been them all. Yet, I know I am completely loved. You have allowed me the room to grow into the women God designed me to be by each being you! I know you've got my back and you are for me, my honey and all my children. This bond is from the giver of every good and perfect gift.

No one does coffee overlooking the lake, bridge jumping, campfire doughnuts, photos at golden hour, prayer and worship nights held in a very poor circle with tears and the Holy Spirit all flowing at the same time like we do! We wade in water while being nibbled by the minnows and eaten by swarms of mosquitos just to get a family photo at the dam. We do ABBA talent night or How the Grinch Who Stole Christmas like we mean it. I hear God's voice better because I've heard Him speak to me through each of you! I love you tons and bunches. What's next year's theme?

Gayle Novak - You are a real pal who is easy to be with and my buddy. Buddy Time partner not only because of the episodes we've done for "the real deal" podcast but because of the way you see into my heart like you've got X-ray vision. Everyone needs a buddy like that. You have a way to speak into a person and filet a tender heart and expose what needs to be seen, removed or prayed over. You are deep and wide, funny and profound. I like to spend time with you and hope our mansions are next to each other in Heaven. I miss you! Let's plan a time together soon!

To my MCBIB family. Paul, Nancy, Bill, Jill, Paul, Janet, Vinod and Shanthini. Thanks for the years of praying for Michael and me, our marriage, grown kids and for loving and supporting the ministry and hunger God has birthed in me...from website design with continued updates, six a.m. morning coffee/counseling sessions, wedding prep or potlucks and pontoon sunset cruises you each support and love so well. God sees! Hey, let's pray sometime or walk Retzer Nature Center!

Jill Briscoe - I recall years ago I sat in your office and gave you a copy of my first book Lily Pads-Stories of God on Display. You graciously received my gift with an inscription made out to you. As you put the book back into the gift bag, you said, "Rachel you should write a devotional next, they're all the rage now!"
That was years ago and "He Speaks" doesn't fit into to the exact mold of a devotional, it's more of an equipping than devotional book. But you've never fit into any mold and that's what I love about you. Thanks for being such a pioneer in my life by telling the truth with a voice of an Englishwoman who has a heart for God. Thanks for allowing me to do the "drop ins" or "pop overs" and have tea with you. Let's tell our goofy stories for "the real deal"
podcast audience again soon. I love to spend time together. I glean so much wisdom from you and I have loads of fun at the same time!

Wisconsin girlfriends...you are the best!
Jeanne Kolb my walking and prayer partner you taught me to love a dog. That's no small feat. I sure did love Gabe! Thanks for being a cheerleader during this book release.

Dana MacNamee, Julie Radtke, Susie Cockle, Elizabeth Cole, Linda Holmberg...You've each prayed for me and listened to me as I verbally process! Yikes! Thank you! I celebrate the new areas you are all exploring and flourishing...each in your own spheres of influence. I'm surrounded by greatness! I miss our together times!

The Pennsylvania dynamic duo - Lisa Dorr and Tabitha Deller...you have the gift of ministering in ways that I can't touch. I celebrate the way you love and serve women only after you love and serve your family. You make me want to move out East. I'm tempted! I prophecy some ministry together in our futures. You are a delight to the body of Christ and you make me giggle so much I'm afraid I'll wet my pants. Let's talk about: knowing or being "Wonder-Woman," wearing each others' product T-shirts, feeding all the stray kitty cats in all of Pennsylvania, swimming pool chats, cute leather earrings-shaped like feathers, holding books upside down during photo shoots, or maybe seeing a Randy Clark look a-like or how about TEETH...Smile Club or Invisalign clear braces...should we? I love you dearly! Come visit me!

To the Bible study group fondly called PIGMENTS... Kent and Lisa Primrose, John and Cheryl Grams, Peter and Anne Mueller, Frank and Renee Notch, Tom and Kirsten Tunnicliff, Dave and Suzie Stuedemann...we are quite a crew! We began our time all in one neighborhood and started in the book of James. Wow! You've been there and had a front row seat for the trial of my life. I've counted it all joy - I wouldn't have made it without you. We've rotated homes and allowed each other in. We been bowling and walked along the shores of Door Country together and you've also walked on the shore of my life and my growth includes your footprints. It's funny all the things we've done together: hours spent at the bonfire and hot tubs at "The Hiding Place" where we were served each meal as if we were the Crawleys of Downtown Abby! We have laughed together, played football on the lawn, assembled puzzles, prayed, studied the Bible and eaten way too much chocolate! Okay, that last part was just me! You have been supportive whether by praying for me in speaking or while writing. I'm grateful you've intersected my path for such at time as this. I hope you know how lavishly loved you are!

Peter and Anne Mueller - you are generous with your love and resources and open with your lives. We love you. You are not only our movie night buddies you've become dear friends. We have a three trailer rule for a reason. Michael is popping the popcorn so come on over. Unless you'd rather swing by Kiltie Drive In for some ice cream. Also...Anne I'd study, explore and process almost anything along side you! So what's next?

Rachel

Rachel Inouye is the author of Lily Pads-Stories of God on Display and host of "the real deal" podcast, a speaker, storyteller, worshipper and blogger, who loves, "Helping people celebrate their significance and the genius of God in them!" Rachel enjoys all things people, walks, dark chocolate and thrifting. She relishes a belly laugh, healthy food and worship music. She desires to usher in hope and encourage others, to be spotted holding hands with her husband Michael and spend time with their amazing kids. She grew up in Iowa and is the youngest of four sisters. For more, check out rachelinouye.org.

Here are some other resources available for you to consider. If they can help you grow in your intimacy with God in any way, I'd be thrilled.

Connect with Rachel:

Lily Pads- Stories of God on Display available on Amazon

"the real deal" podcast: available on iTunes or wherever you listen.

https://podcasts.apple.com/us/podcast/the-real-deal/id1448869614

Blog - Fresh Perspectives on Every Day Life www.rachelinouye.org/blog

Contact Rachel for speaking at your event.
Website: rachelinouye.org
email: rachel@rachelinouye.org

YouTube Channel: rachelinouye.org

I'm Listening

The Companion Journal for He Speaks

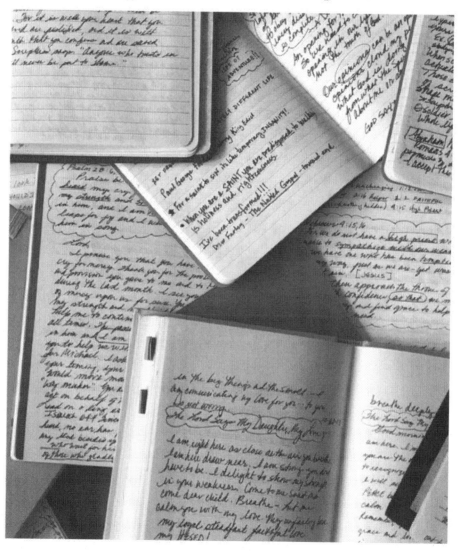

Rachel Inouye

Made in the USA
Columbia, SC
27 September 2020